D1196216

NEWLY DISCOVERED PLANETS

IS THERE POTENTIAL FOR LIFE?

CORONA BREZINA

ROSEN
PUBLISHING

NEW YORK

Published in 2016 by The Rosen Publishing Group, Inc.
29 East 21st Street, New York, NY 10010

Library of Congress Cataloging-in-Publication Data
Brezina, Corona.
 Newly discovered planets : is there potential for life? / Corona Brezina.
    pages cm. -- (The search for other Earths)
 Audience: Grades 7-12.
 Includes bibliographical references and index.
 ISBN 978-1-4994-6295-1 (library bound)
 1. Life on other planets. 2. Extrasolar planets. I. Title.
 QB54.B735 2016
 523.2'4--dc23

                                                          2015025516

Manufactured in China

CONTENTS

Kepler-22b

Kepler-69c

s there anybody out there? Are there any extraterrestrial beings out there in deep space, that is, with their origins beyond the planet Earth? Human beings have speculated for centuries about the possibility of living creatures existing on other planets. In the nineteenth century, conjectures about an advanced civilization existing on Mars, for example, were

Since the beginning of the twenty-first century, some exoplanets have been discovered that are similar to Earth in terms of size and other factors.

52b

Kepler-62f

Kepler-186f

Earth

considered rational scientific hypotheses. Today, advances in scientific knowledge have forced human beings to look further out into the universe in the search for life, and modern technology and instruments are making the search possible.

In 1961, astronomer Frank Drake devised an equation that estimated the number of advanced civilizations in the galaxy. It lays out some of the parameters believed to be important in the potential evolution of intelligent life. These include the rate of formation of stars that could support intelligent life, the number of such stars with planetary systems, the number of planets in each system that could support life, the number of such planets that *actually* support life, the incidence of the development of intelligent life, the number of civilizations that send communications into space, and the typical life span of such a civilization.

The Drake Equation isn't meant to be solved numerically—it's impossible for scientists to determine the value of some of the terms. There's no way that human beings could estimate the typical life span of an alien civilization. And back in 1961, scientists could only speculate about the possible existence of planets orbiting distant stars.

Today, such planets have been proven a reality. Instead of hunting for aliens, scientific efforts are being concentrated on identifying possible faraway planets that could harbor life.

Planets existing outside of the solar system are called exoplanets. Since the first inhospitable exoplanets were detected in the 1990s, astronomers have moved closer to finding distant worlds that resemble Earth more closely.

The exciting new exoplanet discoveries have raised another question: how unique is the Earth? Billions of stars in the galaxy are believed to have at least one planet in the habitable zone where life could conceivably exist. On the other hand, however, the development of complex life-forms on Earth depended on a number of factors. Earth is just the right size and distance from the sun to support liquid water. Its atmospheric makeup creates a hospitable climate that protects life from harmful radiation from the sun. It has magnetic fields, geological activity, and a stabilizing effect from the moon. Which of these factors—if any—are essential to the development of life, and then the evolution of intelligent life?

Scientists are optimistic about the prospect of detecting signs of alien life. In 2015, chief scientist Ellen Stofan at the National Aeronautics and Space Administration (NASA) estimated that humans would find indications of life by 2025 and direct evidence ten to twenty years later. She stated, "We know where to look. We know how to look. In most cases we have the technology, and we're on a path to implementing it," as quoted on Space.com. Most likely, the first alien life-forms detected would be microbes within the solar system. But technology and human ingenuity will also continue to acquire new knowledge of distant exoplanets and bring humans closer to identifying signs of life far from home.

CHAPTER ONE

SEARCHING FOR A PLACE LIKE HOME

Astronomers have identified various exoplanets that are both exotic and similar in some ways to Earth, but they have not yet detected that ultimate goal, the "twin Earth." This hypothetical world would be about the same size and rocky composition as Earth. It would have liquid water and continents. In science fiction books and movies, worlds of this type host plants and animals similar to those on Earth. In real life, it's difficult to determine the properties of planets many light-years away that can't even be directly photographed in most cases.

Life exists on Earth as a result of a very specific set of conditions. If circumstances had been slightly different, living organisms could

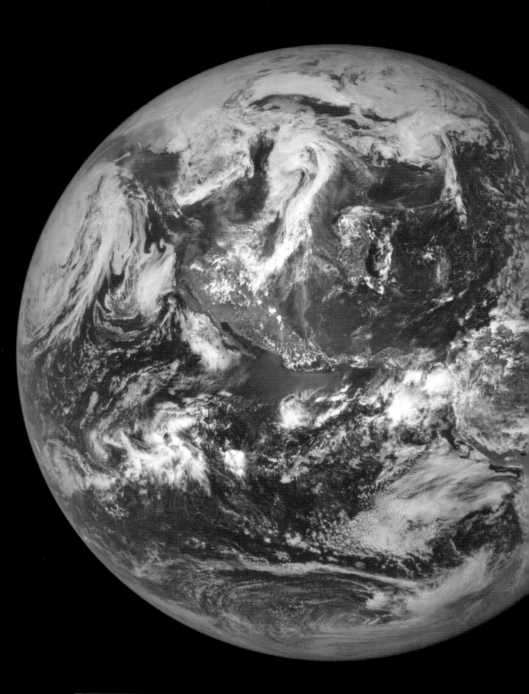

A satellite view taken 1 million miles (1.6 million kilometers) away from Earth shows oceans, continents, and clouds—features that may or may not exist on faraway exoplanets.

have followed a different path of development or might never have come into existence at all. Understanding Earth's unique characteristics, as well as data on other objects in the solar system, can help scientists in their search for planets in other star systems that could support life.

THE HABITABLE ZONE

To be habitable, a planet's orbit must occur within a range that allows the chemistry of life. This set of parameters is sometimes informally referred to as the "Goldilocks Zone," meaning that it is not too hot and not too cold. The term is a huge simplification because the survival of life-forms depends on many factors other than temperature. The scientific description of the habitable zone has evolved over the years, reflecting new theories and discoveries.

Scientists generally consider liquid water to be critical for sustaining life. Bodies of water provide a stable environment for life-forms to exist in and evolve. Most molecules that make up living organisms are soluble in

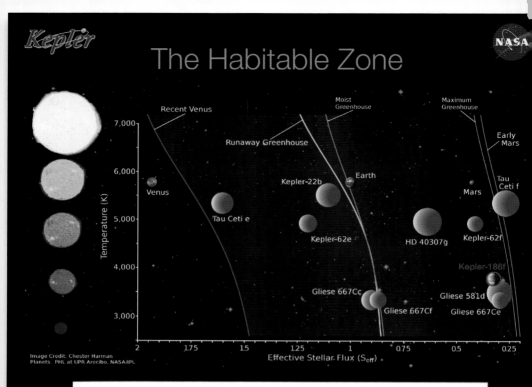

Image Credit: Chester Harman
Planets: PHL at UPR Arecibo, NASA/IPL

Discovered in 2014, Kepler-186f (bottom right) was the first Earth-sized exoplanet found orbiting a star in that star's habitable zone.

water. Usually, the habitable zone is considered to promote conditions that allow liquid water to pool on the planet's surface, but reservoirs of water underneath the surface could also sustain life. Even if water is not an absolute requirement for life to arise, exoplanets supporting liquid water are a good starting point in the search for life because water is believed to be prevalent across the universe.

A planet's potential for habitability depends on the properties of both the planet itself and the star it orbits. The planet must receive the precise amount of light from the star so that it will neither freeze water nor boil it off the surface. Every planetary system will have a habitable zone that is a different distance from the star, depending on the star's size. A star that is significantly larger than the sun would have a habitable zone much farther out in space than Earth's distance from the sun. Giant stars may be less likely than medium sized stars like the sun to create conditions ideal for the evolution of life. Because of their relatively short life span, their orbiting planets simply may not exist long enough for life to take hold.

A planet would probably need to have a nearly circular orbit—not elliptical—to support life. Otherwise, the temperature variations from the nearest to the farthest points of orbit would be too great for life to survive. Similarly, life would be less likely to arise in a system where a planet orbited a double star or existed within a multiple star system, in which the amount of light received would vary depending on the planet's position.

Other factors, in addition to distance from the star, affect a planet's likelihood of sustaining life. Potential suitability for life depends on the planet's size, composition, atmospheric makeup, and surface pressure. It is unlikely that life would arise on a gas giant planet. In seeking twin Earth planets in particular, there are further considerations, such as tides, geologic process, the rate of spin around its axis, and interactions with other objects in the planetary system.

EXTREME LIFE

Discoveries made close to home have caused scientists to expand their definition of the habitable zone. In many places on Earth, life-forms have been found to exist in places that lack some of the criteria once deemed essential for the survival of any type of organism. Some of these places resemble the conditions present across the planet before the emergence of life. They give scientists an opportunity to study the basic processes of the formation of living things. They also could hold clues about how extraterrestrial life could evolve in conditions far different from Earth's environment.

Organisms have been found living in the driest places in the world and in hot springs with water temperatures near the boiling point. They live in environments deep underground, in water ten times saltier than seawater, inside nearly solid rock, and in cold ocean waters at temperatures near zero degrees. Organisms have been identified that can withstand high doses of radiation, a lack of oxygen, and the high pressures of the deep ocean that would kill human beings.

One intriguing form of life exists in hydro-thermal vents on the sea floor. Ocean water undergoes chemical reactions when it seeps through the rocky bottom and is heated by magma near the surface. It then gushes forth from the vents as a hot fluid—as high as 750°F (400°C) in temperature—that is rich in minerals. The life-forms that exist around these vents survive extreme pressure, extreme heat,

Gases bubble up from a hydrothermal vent near Papua New Guinea, in the South Pacific Ocean. A sulfur crust can be seen surrounding the vent.

a lack of sunlight, and environmental conditions that would be toxic to most organisms. Consequently, vent life-forms have developed unique metabolic processes. Some microbes utilize chemical energy directly in a process called chemosynthesis as an alternative to photosynthesis, which requires sunlight. They survive through a chemical reaction that uses hydrogen sulfide to drive their metabolisms.

PLANETARY NEIGHBORS

The solar system consists of four small inner planets and four outer gas giants. The gas giants, which are Jupiter, Saturn, Uranus, and Neptune, are considered uninhabitable. Of the four rocky inner planets, Venus and Mars fall just outside of the habitable zone. Nonetheless, their unsuitability for life stems from additional factors along with their distance from the sun. A comparison of Venus, Earth, and Mars can contribute to an understanding of how three close planetary neighbors can evolve into very different worlds.

Historically, scientists speculated that Venus and Mars could someday be found to harbor life. Scientists discovered in the late eighteenth century that Venus had an atmosphere, and they wondered whether there could be life-forms under the blanket of clouds. In the late nineteenth century, astronomers observing Mars thought that they had glimpsed canals, perhaps created by advanced civilizations. Missions launched during the twentieth century disproved both theories.

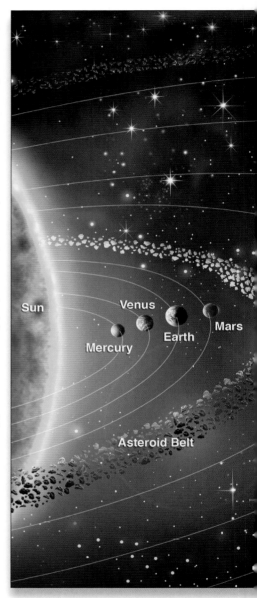

Comets

Neptune

Uranus

Saturn

ter

The solar system consists of four small rocky planets, two gas giants, two ice giants, and innumerable smaller bodies, all held in orbit by the gravitational pull of the sun.

Venus is sometimes called Earth's sister planet for its similarities in size, mass, composition, and gravity. It is now known, however, that Venus is the hottest planet in the solar system; its 860°F (460°C) average surface temperature is hot enough to melt lead. The atmosphere of Venus, consisting of carbon dioxide gas blanketed with clouds of sulfuric acid, is the thickest among any of the planets, and its surface contains very little water. The high temperature is caused by the greenhouse effect of the carbon dioxide trapping the heat delivered by sunlight.

Scientists generally agree that Venus supported liquid water on its surface early in its development. At some point, its oceans were lost in space as the water molecules broke into hydrogen and oxygen gas. Scientists do not altogether agree on how long the oceans existed—as little as six hundred million years or as long as two billion years. Further research into Venus's history will help scientists differentiate whether a faraway exoplanet exists within the habitable zone or on the fringe, where conditions would be more likely to resemble those of Venus.

Mars, in contrast, is only half the size of Earth. It has a thin atmosphere and an average temperature of -67°F (-55°C). Nevertheless, this cold desert world is viewed as the most promising neighbor in the solar system for identifying traces of life. Although the theoretical canals seen by nineteenth-century astronomers proved to be optical illusions, some of Mars's surface features could have been formed by liquid water long ago.

Today, the thin atmosphere of Mars cannot sustain surface water, although the planet has polar ice caps. Exploratory missions have indicated that Mars may have been a warmer, wetter planet in the past. Some scientists believe that life could have arisen under these circumstances. Now, the oceans are long gone, either vaporized and lost in space or locked inside the planet, in the form of ice or liquid water. If Mars ever supported life, missions such as the Mars Exploration Rovers could someday find fossil evidence on

NASA's *Curiosity* Mars rover drills into a sandstone target with a laser, collecting samples for analysis, in a 2014 self-portrait.

the planet's surface. Conceivably, simple organisms such as microbes could still exist, probably hidden away under the surface.

AMAZING MOONS

The outer gas giants in the solar system are not considered capable of sustaining life, but they are orbited by numerous rocky moons. The physical properties

FLYBYS AND ROVERS

In 1962, NASA's Mariner 2 mission to Venus became the first unmanned space probe to reach another planet in the solar system. Data collected by its instruments revealed that there was no chance that any life-form could survive Venus's hot surface temperature. In 1965, the Mariner 4 mission achieved a flyby of Mars and sent back the first photographs of the planet's surface. The images of its barren rocky terrain dashed any hopes that Earth's nearest neighbor was the home of living creatures inhabiting an Earth-like environment.

Since then, NASA has redirected its search for life in the solar system toward simpler organisms. The Mars Exploration Rover missions were sent to study the climate, geology, and potential habitability of the planet. The rover *Curiosity* (of the Mars Science Laboratory mission, which is part of the Mars Exploration Rover program), which touched down in 2012, has confirmed that the chemistry on Mars could once have supported life long ago.

How could humans ever have any hope of identifying microscopic life-forms on worlds such as the moons of the outer planets, which are hundreds of millions of miles away? Flyby exploration missions yield data on faraway environmental conditions that could conceivably harbor life. The Galileo mission, which lasted from 1989 to 2003, sent back images and data on Jupiter and its moons. The ongoing Cassini mission is studying Saturn and its moons. Follow-up missions will explore features that could potentially support life.

of these moons vary greatly. A few have atmospheres. Despite their vast distances from the sun, scientists believe that a few of them could be capable of harboring simple life-forms. Ultimately, study of these moons could bring about discoveries that could eventually prove useful in the search for life on faraway exoplanets. If frozen moons in our own solar system could give rise to life, similar bodies in other systems could follow the same model.

Scientists have long been fascinated by Jupiter's fourth largest moon, Europa, which is slightly smaller than Earth's moon. All of the outer moons have frigid surface temperatures—Europa never gets any warmer than -260°F (-160C). But the moon is believed to have a liquid ocean of water underneath a frozen layer of ice a couple of miles thick. The surface is marked by cracks that may have been caused by tidal motion of the water. The Hubble Space Telescope has photographed plumes from geysers of water vapor shooting into space, and the icy surface may exhibit plate tectonics similar to the movement of the plates of Earth's

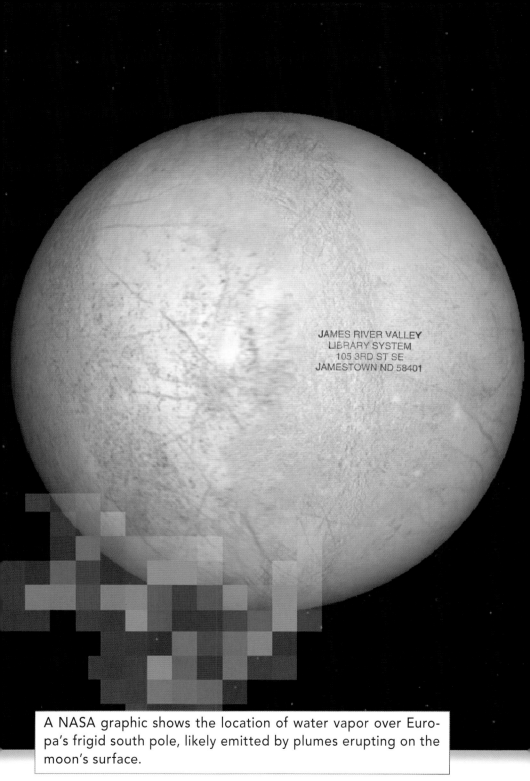

A NASA graphic shows the location of water vapor over Europa's frigid south pole, likely emitted by plumes erupting on the moon's surface.

crust. Scientists believe that Europa's ocean may be salty, meaning that it could contain key compounds necessary for the biology of life.

Two of Jupiter's other large moons, Ganymede and Callisto, may also possess vast oceans beneath their cold surfaces. Ganymede, which is almost the size of Mars, is the largest moon in the solar system. Both moons have icy, cratered crusts that exhibit less geologic activity than Europa, and Callisto is sometimes described as a dead world. Their oceans would occur much deeper than Europa's oceans—liquid water would be buried at least 60 miles (100 km).

An artist's illustration shows a geyser of water erupting on the surface of Enceladus, with Saturn on the horizon in the background.

In 2014, observations revealed that Saturn's moon Enceladus could have a huge ocean underlying its south pole. Enceladus is a tiny moon, just over 300 miles (500 km) in diameter. Scientists find Enceladus interesting because of the geysers erupting from the pole to a height of 125 miles (200 km). Analysis showed that the water released contains salts and some of the compounds essential to life. Scientists are particularly intrigued by the possibility that hydrothermal activity could occur at the bottom of the ocean, raising the possibility of hydrothermal vents hosting exotic forms of life.

Saturn's huge moon Titan, which is nearly the size of Mars, resembles Earth in some ways. It has a thick atmosphere, lakes, rivers, clouds, and rain. But at its average temperature of -290°F (-180°C), Titan's liquid water and clouds are made up of methane (natural gas) and ethane. It is possible that a liquid ocean exists under the moon's surface. Scientists do not believe that life-forms similar to those on Earth could exist on Titan, but the moon's complex organic chemistry makes it unique in the solar system.

It might seem hard to believe that liquid oceans could exist within celestial bodies so far away from the sun, and scientists are still studying the heat sources of these moons. Tidal forces are one significant factor. Europa, for example, is affected by the huge gravitational force of Jupiter as well as its neighboring moons. The tidal pull from these bodies causes the moon to flex, generating heat that keeps the interior ocean liquid. Some scientists believe that the oceans of Europa and a couple of the other moons could each contain more water than exists on the entire Earth.

EXAMINING THE SOLAR SYSTEM

The solar system is made up of much more than the sun, moon, and planets. There are objects such as dwarf planets, asteroids, and comets that also orbit the sun. These bodies can interact with one another, either through gravitational forces or collision.

In addition, the entire solar system exists inside an unseen bubble called the heliosphere.

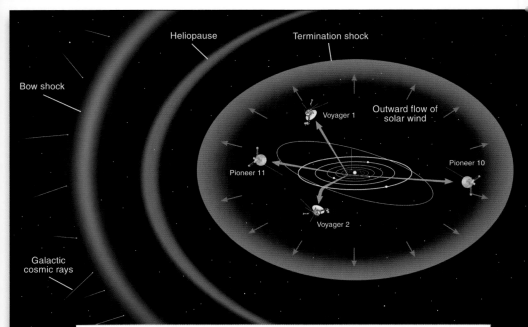

The heliosphere extends far beyond the orbit of the planets in the solar system. Shown here are NASA spacecraft that are bound for interstellar space.

It is created by the solar wind, which is the stream of particles and fields streaming from the sun. The radiation in space, mostly generated by the sun, is more intense than on Earth, where the atmosphere protects life-forms by filtering out most harmful rays. In other solar systems, especially those orbiting stars larger than the sun, the radiation could be much stronger.

People generally view the possibility of a collision with an asteroid or comet as potentially catastrophic, but such events transformed the young planet Earth. Asteroids and comets were the original source of all of Earth's water. Asteroid and comet strikes also may have brought the organic compounds necessary for life. Researchers running experiments on the International Space Station have found that microbes can survive the conditions of the vacuum of space, and they believe that life could probably survive on asteroids as well. Some scientists have even speculated that primordial life could originally have had its origin in space debris.

CHAPTER TWO

IDENTIFYING THE FIRST EXOPLANETS

A stronomers began searching for exoplanets in the mid-twentieth century. Scientists had long suspected that stars other than the sun would host their own solar systems. Abundant material for the formation of planets occurs across the galaxy, and there was no reason to believe that our own solar system was a unique phenomenon.

Observations of faraway worlds proved a challenge for astronomers, however. Even the sun's closest neighboring stars lie so far away that distances between them are measured in light-years rather than miles or kilometers. In addition, exoplanets orbit close to stars that dwarf them in size and brightness. A telescope pointed at a star with an exoplanet would probably not be able to glimpse it because of the star's intense light close by.

Therefore, astronomers must generally detect exoplanets through indirect means. Researchers recognized this decades ago and attempted to identify anomalies in their observations of stars that could indicate the existence of an exoplanet. Only in the late twentieth century, however, did advances in instrumentation and technology allow the definitive identification of faraway exoplanets.

HOW TO DETECT AN EXOPLANET

Planets interact with the star they're orbiting. Their gravitational forces tug at the star as they move in space. As the planet passes in front of its star, it affects the star's apparent brightness to observers. Scientists are able to detect planets by observing how they affect their star. Several different methods can identify exoplanets and yield data on their characteristics.

One method of detection is the transit method. The transit method is the means used

The Kepler mission, which launched the Kepler Space Telescope in 2009, was NASA's first mission capable of identifying exoplanets that are the same size as Earth.

by the Kepler Space Telescope. Because the Kepler mission has identified the largest number of known exoplanets, it has proven to be the most successful method so far.

A transit occurs when one celestial body is observed to pass in front of another when viewed from Earth. When a faraway planet passes in front of the face of its star, the light from the star is slightly dimmed. Sensitive instruments can monitor a star's brightness for this telltale dimming and determine its orbit and size, but not its mass.

Another method is called the radial velocity, or Doppler, method of detection. Before the Kepler mission, the greatest number of exoplanets had been identified using the radial velocity method. This method takes advantage of the fact that a planet's gravitational pull causes a star to move slightly, in a tiny circle or ellipse, as the planet orbits. "Radial velocity" refers to a star's velocity, or speed, toward and away from the observer. Scientists can determine whether a star is moving toward Earth or away from it by examining its spectrum—the pattern of light emitted by a star. The tiny periodic change in the star's motion due to the gravitational pull of a planet causes the spectrum to shift. For a star moving toward Earth, the light is shifted toward the blue end of the spectrum; for a star moving away from Earth, it moves back toward the red end. Because larger planets have a greater gravitational pull than smaller ones, the radial velocity method is best at detecting big planets. It can provide some data on the planet's mass and orbit, but not its size. A set of observations using both the radial

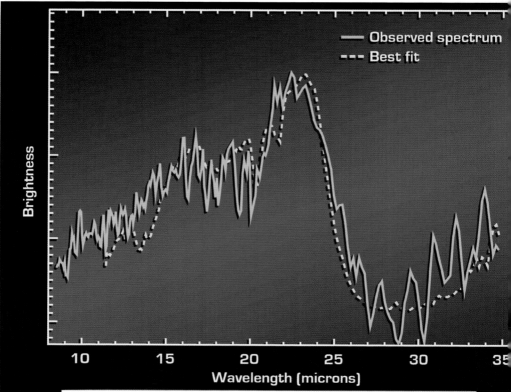

By examining spectra of light, astronomers can identify the makeup of distant objects in space. This spectrum, taken by the Spitzer Space Telescope, contains a signature for silicate dust.

velocity method and the transit method can provide more information on the planet than either method on its own.

A couple of other methods have been used to detect a small number of exoplanets. The gravitational microlensing method observes the magnification of the star's light caused by the planet's gravitational field—this is a different effect from the gravitational pull. The

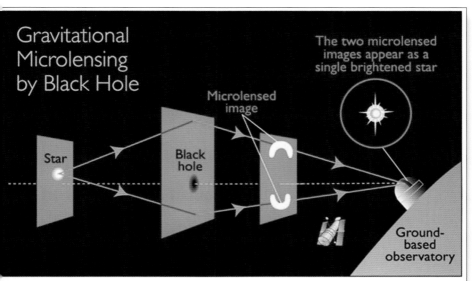

Gravitational Microlensing by Black Hole

Microlensed image

Star

Black hole

The two microlensed images appear as a single brightened star

Ground-based observatory

he intense gravitational field of a fore-round black hole acts like a powerful lens space. In the diagram, the black hole "lens" istorts and brightens the image of a back-round star. The gravitational lens smears ıe star's image into two banana-shaped ınages with a total surface area several mes that of the original stellar disk.

Though the angular separation is shown here, it is 100 times smaller than what HST can resolve. Hence the phenomenon is called "microlensing." HST and other telescopes instead see a brightening of the star as the black hole drifts by, but they do not resolve the multiple images.

ISON AGENCY

Stars can also act as gravitational lenses. If the lensing star has an exoplanet, it can be identified through observations of its contributions to the lensing effect.

gravitational microlensing method has not yielded many finds, but it is capable of iden-tifying small planets that are very far away. Another method, the timing method, makes observations of variations that the presence of a planet causes in a periodic phenomenon. In the transit timing variation method, for exam-ple, astronomers can detect an additional planet or group of planets in a system by observing variations in the timing of a planet transiting a star.

Direct imaging—observation of the planet itself—became possible in the 2000s. Specialized optical equipment and ingenious photographic methods have produced direct images of a handful of exoplanets. One successful method involves blocking out the star so that a telescope can capture light received from the planet. Direct imaging is still in its early stages, but the technique has the potential to collect data about the planets that cannot be acquired through other methods. Spectra obtained from the planet's light can offer information such as temperature, composition, and properties of its atmosphere.

Most of these methods of exoplanet detection are fallible in one way or another. In the transit method, for example, a planet will not be detected unless it is seen to pass in front of the face of its star. The radial velocity method can also miss some planets depending on their position and size.

THE FIRST DISCOVERIES

In 1992, Aleksander Wolszczan and Dale Frail made the first definitive exoplanet identification. They were observing a pulsar, a dense remnant of a star that reached the end of its life and exploded as a supernova. Pulsars rotate very rapidly and emit beams of radiation that can be observed as regular pulses. The pair of astronomers weren't specifically hunting for planets, but they noticed a slight unevenness to the pulses. The signals would occur closer together and then farther apart than expected. For some reason, the pulsar was being tugged in one direction and then in another. The astronomers determined that two planets were orbiting the pulsar and affecting its motion. The planets are now known to each be about four times the mass of Earth.

If people had imagined that the first exoplanets found could resemble Earth, they were disappointed. There is no chance that they could harbor life because conditions around a pulsar are extremely inhospitable.

The first identification of planets orbiting a sunlike star also provided a surprise. In 1995, astronomers Michel Mayor and Didier Queloz used the radial velocity method to detect a planet orbiting the star 51 Pegasus. The exoplanet, 51 Pegasi b, was a giant half the size of

Exoplanet 51 Pegasi b, shown here in an artist's conception, orbits a star forty-two light-years away. The hot giant's surface temperature is probably about 1800°F (1000°C).

Jupiter. It moved in a very fast, tight orbit around its star—a year on the planet lasts slightly more than the equivalent of four days on Earth. The distance between the exoplanet and its star was much closer than Earth's distance from the sun. Once again, the newly discovered planet had little in common with Earth. It belongs to a type now referred to as a "hot Jupiter."

In 1999, the first multiple planet system was discovered, around the star Upsilon Andromedae. The trio of planets—a fourth has since been identified—are all comparable in size to Jupiter and orbit relatively close to their star.

"HOT JUPITERS" AND NEW QUESTIONS

By 2000, astronomers had found about thirty exoplanets. New milestones continued to take place. In 2001, astronomers detected the first planet believed to fall within the habitable zone of its star. Identified as HD 28185 b, the giant is six times the mass of Jupiter. In 2002, the first "cold Jupiter" was discovered. Unlike the many

FALSE IDENTIFICATIONS

In 1995, when astronomers announced the discovery of 51 Pegasi b to the American Astronomical Society, some scientists were skeptical of the claim. The planet, a hot Jupiter orbiting close to its star, defied expectations. In addition, there had been plenty of false detections in the past.

The hunt for exoplanets began back in the 1940s. In the 1960s, an astronomer announced the detection of planets around Barnard's Star, the fourth closest neighbor to the sun. The claim was later discredited as an instrument error. A couple of separate promising observations around other stars were also shown to be false. In 1988, a team announced a possible planetary system around gamma Cephei, but they retracted the claim in 1992. (A 2002 observation confirmed the existence of a planet orbiting the star.)

The misidentifications led some astronomers to believe that searching for exoplanets was a hopeless quest. In 1991, an astronomer was poised to announce the discovery of a planet around a pulsar. A week before the 1992 presentation, however, he recognized an error in his calculations. Instead of announcing an exoplanet, he publicly retracted the claim before the audience. Soon afterward, however, a separate detection of a pair of planets around a different pulsar was confirmed, ushering in the exoplanet era.

hot giants discovered, it orbited at about the same distance from its star as Jupiter from the sun. In 2007, the first temperature map of an exoplanet was produced. The hot Jupiter HD 189733 b had a hot spot on its surface and exhibited ferocious easterly winds. By 2008, the number of known exoplanets had exceeded three hundred.

Before the discovery of the first exoplanets, scientists had theorized that faraway planetary

The hot Jupiter type exoplanet HD 15082 b, shown in this computer artwork, is hotter than some stars. It orbits its star in just 1.2 days.

systems would resemble the known solar system. But the early discoveries belied this prediction. Most of the new exoplanets were the "hot Jupiter" types—large gas giants orbiting closer to their star than the distance at which Mercury travels around the sun. They are now believed to form further away from their stars but gradually move closer, although not so

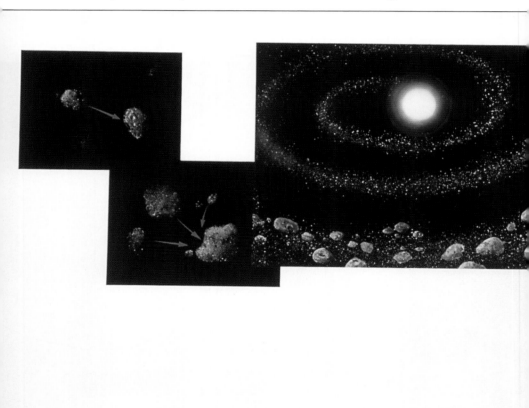

close that they are pulled in by their star's gravity. Some of these planets have highly irregular orbits. Instead of circling the star's equator, they may orbit at a tilt to the star. They are also tidally locked, meaning that a planet's dayside facing the sun can be over a thousand degrees hotter than the nightside. The giant hot Jupiters were considered highly unlikely to be suitable for life.

According to the core accretion theory, the Earth and other bodies in the solar system coalesced from particles of dust. Many exoplanets, however, cannot be explained by this theory.

The nature of these planets and planetary systems surprised scientists. Even the planets identified as types other than hot Jupiters defied expectations. Some had highly eccentric orbits, meaning that they do not revolve in a perfect circle centered around the star. How could such bizarre new discoveries have formed? Scientists were forced to reevaluate their theory on how planetary systems come into existence.

The standard model, based on the solar system, was the core accretion model. Scientists hypothesized that planets were created out of material left over from the formation of a star. This material coalesced into a flattened, spinning disk, and it began to clump together to form larger objects. The innermost material tended to be rocky, since the lighter gases had been incorporated into the star. These bands yielded the small inner planets. Farther out, the larger planets were formed out of water and gases as well as rocky material. The final result was a system orbiting in almost perfect circles on the same plane. If a hot Jupiter had migrated inward during the formation of the solar system, it probably would not have allowed the formation or survival of the inner planets.

Eventually scientists determined that "hot Jupiters" were not the most common type of exoplanet. They were merely the easiest to detect because of their size and proximity to their stars. Nonetheless, subsequent discoveries unveiled such a diversity of planetary systems that the core accretion theory has been refuted as a standard model. The template for the solar system doesn't match the observations of other systems, and scientists are currently exploring new models that could explain the findings. Still, exoplanet detection methods are not particularly effective at finding systems made up of both large and small planets. Further discoveries will yield more data that will reveal whether or not the solar system really is unusual among planetary systems.

MORE EYES IN THE SKY

The rapid advances in exoplanet detection were largely made possible by new space telescopes. These instruments yield sharper images than land-based telescopes because the clarity is not distorted by Earth's atmosphere. The era began with the Hubble Space Telescope (HST), launched in 1990. The HST has discovered many exoplanets using the transit method of detection. In 2001, the HST probed the atmosphere of an exoplanet for the first time using an instrument called a spectroscope. Light from a star passing through the atmosphere of the exoplanet during a transit can be captured by the spectroscope, revealing details of the planet's

For nearly twenty-five years, observations by the Hubble Space Telescope have enabled many exciting breakthroughs in astronomy, including contributions in identifying and understanding exoplanets.

atmospheric makeup. Traces of sodium were detected in the atmosphere of gas giant HD 209458 b. In 2008, the HST detected the first presence of an organic molecule—methane—on the same exoplanet.

In 2003, NASA launched the Spitzer Space Telescope, which had infrared capabilities that allowed viewing objects too dim for ordinary telescopes. In 2005, the Spitzer Space Telescope observed direct light emitted by exoplanets for the first time. In 2007, Spitzer made the first detection of water vapor on HD 189733 b, a hot Jupiter exoplanet.

In 2006, France launched the Convection, Rotation and planetary Transits (COROT) space telescope. It was the first mission dedicated to the study of exoplanets. It identified its first planet, the hot Jupiter dubbed COROT-1, in 2007, using the transit method. In 2009, COROT detected the smallest exoplanet known up to that time, about twice the size of Earth. COROT-7b was also the first rocky exoplanet discovered, with a density close to that of Earth. The new world was still not close to being a twin Earth, however. It orbits its star very closely, and scientists now speculate that it is the remnant of a former gas giant.

In addition, detection of new planets has been aided by advances in instruments and in computer power and tools. Land-based telescopes, including the Nordic Optical Telescope on the island of La Palma, Spain, are also used to confirm identification and obtain more data on exoplanets.

CHAPTER THREE

THE PLANET HUNTING MISSION

I n 2009, NASA launched the Kepler mission, which was designed specifically to detect exoplanets. In particular, scientists hoped that it would identify planets the size of Earth and smaller in the habitable zone, allowing a determination of how common these types of worlds are.

The $600 million mission was very low-cost compared to other NASA missions. The 2,300-pound (1,000-kg) spacecraft consisted of little more than a telescope and a camera.

Unlike the Hubble Space Telescope and most other man-made satellites, the Kepler spacecraft orbits around the sun instead of Earth. Scientists made this choice so that Earth would not block Kepler's view of its target patch of the cosmos. It

A Delta 2 rocket lifts off from a launch pad in Cape Canaveral, Florida, on March 6, 2009, carrying the Kepler satellite into space.

also keeps the spacecraft clear of stray light and Earth's gravitational fluctuations. Kepler orbits more slowly than Earth, and the spacecraft will not near Earth again until 2070. Because Kepler quickly moved away from the vicinity of Earth after the launch, making repair attempts would be impossible if malfunctions occurred.

THE KEPLER MISSION

Kepler's mission was to continuously monitor the brightness of all the stars in one field of view. It was trained on a small patch of sky in the constellation Cygnus, which residents of North America can see in the summer. The area, which contains an arm of the Milky Way, is about the same size as twenty full moons. NASA planned for Kepler to constantly scan the brightness of the stars in its field of view, which included more than 150,000 total of the same type of star as the sun. After the first year, the number would be narrowed down to about 100,000.

Kepler was unique in being the only space telescope dedicated to detecting exoplanets as a long-term project. The initial mission was planned to last for three and a half years. The lengthy period of time would allow Kepler to identify planets that pass across the face of their stars slowly, unlike the many hot Jupiters that whip around their stars rapidly. The astronomers who were running the mission wanted to observe three transits before announcing that an object was an exoplanet.

NASA laid out a set of objectives in describing the mission:

- Determine the percentage of terrestrial and larger planets that are in or near the habitable zone of a wide variety of stars
- Determine the distribution of sizes and shapes of the orbits of these planets
- Estimate how many planets there are in multiple-star systems
- Determine the variety of orbit sizes and planet reflectivities, sizes, masses, and densities of short-period giant planets
- Identify additional members of each discovered planetary system using other techniques

- Determine the properties of those stars that harbor planetary systems

These goals address a broad range of characteristics of exoplanets and their stars. But to most people, the most tantalizing aspect of the Kepler mission was the possibility of detecting a twin Earth planet. Kepler was not designed to search for life, but it was intended to create a census where future missions might hunt for signs of life.

The Kepler spacecraft quickly began fulfilling its purpose. In August 2009, it confirmed its functionality with a successful detection of a previously identified exoplanet, TrES-2. In January 2010, Kepler's detection of five new hot Jupiters was announced. In mid-2010, Kepler detected an exoplanetary system that was confirmed by the transit timing variation method, making it the first successful identification by that method. One of the three planets in the system also marked the first discovery of a planet in the same size range as Earth. Kepler-9d, which is about 1.6 times the size of Earth, has two gas giants as planetary neighbors. It orbits its star at a very close distance, not in the habitable zone.

Over the next few years, Kepler continued increasing its tally of confirmed exoplanets, transforming scientists' understanding of worlds beyond our own. During the years up to 2008, there were fewer than 100 identifications of exoplanets each year. From 2009 until 2013, there were between 100 and 200 each year, increasingly because of Kepler. In 2014, nearly 900 exoplanets were detected, almost all by Kepler. In 2015, it was announced that Kepler had exceeded its one thousandth identification. As of mid-2015, out of 1,948 known exoplanets, 1,033 had been detected by Kepler.

Kepler's mission was extended in 2012 for another three and a half years, but in May 2013, the spacecraft lost the second of its four reaction wheels. This mechanical problem meant that the telescope could no longer remain pointed at the same patch of sky, which was essential to its original mission. Because Kepler is still basically functional, scientists devised a new mission, dubbed K2, for the spacecraft.

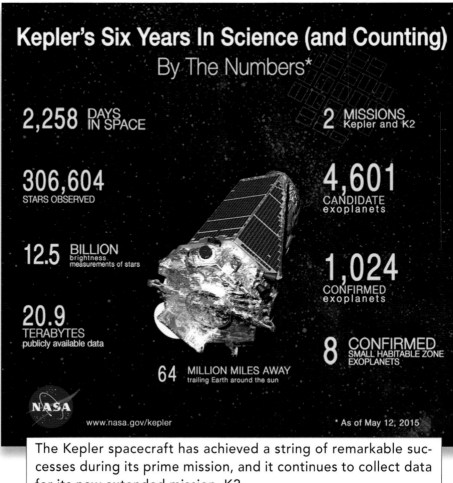

Kepler's Six Years In Science (and Counting)
By The Numbers*

2,258 DAYS IN SPACE

306,604 STARS OBSERVED

12.5 BILLION brightness measurements of stars

20.9 TERABYTES publicly available data

64 MILLION MILES AWAY trailing Earth around the sun

2 MISSIONS Kepler and K2

4,601 CANDIDATE exoplanets

1,024 CONFIRMED exoplanets

8 CONFIRMED SMALL HABITABLE ZONE EXOPLANETS

NASA

www.nasa.gov/kepler

* As of May 12, 2015

The Kepler spacecraft has achieved a string of remarkable successes during its prime mission, and it continues to collect data for its new extended mission, K2.

CATEGORIZING EARTH'S DISTANT NEIGHBORS

Kepler detects exoplanets using the transit method, but the astronomers running the mission present its identifications only as candidates. At that point, an exoplanet detection may turn out to be either a true planet or a false signature. The exoplanet is not considered a positive identification until it is confirmed by another method of detection. A telescope on the ground might make the confirmation using the radial velocity method, for example. Some are confirmed with observations from other space telescopes, such as the Spitzer Space Telescope. Increasingly, the transit timing method has confirmed detections. Nonetheless, because more than 90 percent of Kepler's detections have later been verified, it's a likely assumption that most of Kepler's current candidate planets will eventually be confirmed.

Data from Kepler's observations, often combined with data from the confirming radial velocity method of detection, provide some basic characteristics of exoplanets. Typically, the planet's mass (in some cases), radius, density (in some cases), and temperature can be calculated (mass can be more difficult to measure for smaller planets, and density cannot be calculated without mass). Kepler's data includes the number of days it takes for the planet to orbit

The infrared Spitzer Space Telescope, depicted in front of the Milky Way Galaxy, seeks to answer questions about the origins of the objects and phenomena observed in the universe.

its star, its distance from the star, and the shape of its orbit. Kepler also collects data on the planet's parent star, including its mass, temperature, radius, and metallicity, which is the star's metal content. Metallicity has been shown to be a factor in predicting the type of planets orbiting the star.

Exoplanets are so new to science that there is not yet any official consensus on classifying them into categories. Nevertheless, three broad types of known exoplanets include rocky planets, gas dwarfs, and ice or gas giants. Gas dwarfs are between 1.7 and 3.9 times the size of Earth; giants are

Based on astronomical observations, an artist's conception shows the formation of a young solar system. Gas giants are developing in a gap between an inner and an outer planet-forming disk.

more than 3.9 times the size of Earth. Rocky planets can be large or small. Although planets smaller than about 1.5 the size of Earth are likely to be rocky, there is no upper limit on the size of rocky planets. Another type of categorization differentiates between the hot Jupiters close to the star and the gas giants that occur farther out from the star in eccentric orbits.

The metallicity of the planet's star tends to correlate with the type of planet. A 2014 analysis showed that stars with the same amount of metal content as the sun tended to host planets smaller than 1.7 times the size

The Kepler spacecraft is shown operating in its new K2 mission, which will continue the search for exoplanets and observe a variety of other celestial objects.

of Earth. Stars with high levels of metals were more likely to have gas and ice giants.

One of the most common types of exoplanet detected by Kepler is known as a "super Earth." These planets are larger than Earth but smaller than Neptune, which is about seventeen times the size of Earth. Because they are a newly discovered category of planet, little is known about their characteristics other than their size. The frequency of super Earths came as a surprise to astronomers because this type of mid-size planet does not occur in our solar system. The first super Earths were detected before the launch of Kepler, but Kepler's data has revealed their abundance among exoplanets.

Kepler has demonstrated that it can detect smaller planets as well. One of the smallest exoplanets yet detected is Kepler-37b. With a diameter of 2,400 miles (3,860 km), the rocky little world is about the same size as the moon. The sunlike star also has two slightly larger outer planets. All three exoplanets orbit their star at a distance closer than Mercury's orbit around the sun, putting them in a range too hot to be considered habitable. Another system of planets discovered by Kepler, which is around the dwarf star Kepler-42, consists of three planets, all smaller than Earth.

AMAZING EXOPLANETS

Some exoplanets make headlines because of their potential habitability. Others capture the attention of scientists and the imagination of the public for a variety of different reasons. The following examples are some of the remarkable exoplanets that have been detected, both by the Kepler Space Telescope and other telescopes, including ground-based telescopes:

- The "diamond planet," PSR J1719-1438 b, is an exoplanet with the mass of Jupiter that orbits a pulsar. It's made of carbon but has a density greater than that of diamond.
- Another carbon rich planet, super Earth 55 Cancri e, exhibits drastic atmospheric variability that could be caused by extreme volcanic eruptions.
- The super Earth Gliese 1214b is rich in water, but because of the hot temperature and crushing pressure on the planet, it exists in a plasma state.
- The darkest exoplanet is the gas giant TrES-2b. Blacker than coal, it reflects almost no light, making it a scientific enigma.
- PSO J318.5-22 is a young exoplanet six times the size of Jupiter drifting in space with no host star. Some scientists believe that rogue planets are common, but they are very difficult to detect.

- The puffy planet HAT-P-1 weighs about half as much as Jupiter, but it is about 1.38 times as large in diameter, making it lighter than cork in density.
- Kepler-16b is a cold gas planet that orbits two stars, meaning that it has double sunsets like the fictional planet of Tatooine in *Star Wars*.
- The oldest exoplanets discovered, the system of five small rocky planets orbiting Kepler-444, are11.2 billion years old—80 percent the age of the universe.

BUT IS IT HABITABLE?

With every new notable exoplanet announcement, one of the first questions asked is whether the new world could harbor life. Although Kepler was never meant to detect life directly, one of its primary goals was to locate planets resembling Earth orbiting stars resembling the sun. A small proportion of Kepler's detections have been categorized in the habitable zone.

In addition, some of the telescope's discoveries have raised the question of whether scientists should expand the criteria for habitability. The detection of so many super Earths, in particular, has prompted speculation on whether they could support life. Scientists also continue to debate the definition of the habitable zone. What types of stars are most likely to host exoplanets that are hospitable to life? Could planets existing on the edge of the hypo-thetical habitable zone be more likely to support life than is currently believed? These types of questions and more will continue to be discussed as scientists expand their understand-ing of exoplanets.

In 2011, Kepler made its first detection of a planet identified within the habitable zone. Kepler-22b is a planet slightly

An artist's conception depicts Kepler-22b as a blue ocean world. If the planet does have an atmosphere, its surface temperature could be about the same as that of Earth.

larger than twice the size of Earth. It orbits its sunlike star at a distance slightly less than the distance Earth is from the sun.

As of 2015, about thirty to fifty exoplanets were known to exist within the habitable zone of their system, depending on criteria. These include twelve planets detected by Kepler as being less than twice the size of Earth. Eight of these were announced in January 2015 at the same time that Kepler surpassed its one thousandth detection. Several newly identified Kepler exoplanets bear the closest resemblance to Earth found so far. Many more of Kepler's possible planet candidates are still being evaluated.

The most earthlike of Kepler's discoveries is Kepler-452b, announced in 2015. Described as an older, bigger planetary cousin, the exoplanet is a super Earth about 1,400 light-years away. It orbits a star similar to the sun at about the same distance as Earth. A year lasts 385 days— slightly longer than an Earth year. At 6 billion years old, Kepler-452b is at a later stage of its development than Earth. Although its composition is unknown, scientists consider it probable that it is a rocky planet with a thick atmosphere.

Other 2015 discoveries include the exoplanets Kepler-438b, just 12 percent larger than Earth, and Kepler-442b, 33 percent larger than Earth. Both planets orbit stars that are slightly dimmer than the sun—a red dwarf and an orange dwarf. Because the stars are smaller and cooler than the sun, the habitable zone is closer than Earth's distance from the sun, and a year for these exoplanets is relatively short. Kepler-438b orbits its star in 35 days, and Kepler-442b orbits its star in 112 days. Both exoplanets are believed to fall within the habitable zone. Still, these worlds are not yet true twin Earths and nothing is known about their composition other than that they are likely to be rocky planets.

Many of Kepler's most promising detections orbit red dwarf stars, which make up about 70 percent of the stars in the Milky Way. Astronomers believe that red dwarfs could potentially have habitable planets because the stars are stable and have a long life span.

Discovered in 2007, the exoplanet Gliese 581c is a super Earth about five times more massive than Earth. It is most likely too hot to be habitable.

Two intriguing exoplanets orbiting a red dwarf are Kepler-62e and Kepler-62f, which belong to a five-planet system. Both are less than twice the size of Earth, and they orbit within the habitable zone. Computer models have indicated that these planets could be water worlds with no dry land.

Even as the hunt for life focuses on possible twin Earths, some of the other known exoplanets spark excited speculation about the potential for life on exoplanets that aren't considered ideally habitable by the usual criteria. Some super Earths, for example, could conceivably harbor life. One planetary system that has been intensively studied orbits the red dwarf star Gliese 581. At just twenty light-years away, it's a close neighbor to the sun. In 2007, the exoplanet Gliese 581c, classified as a super Earth, was detected using the radial velocity detection method. Some scientists believe that the surface atmosphere of Gliese 581c is very hot, similar to that of Venus. In 2009, the super Earth exoplanet Gliese 581d was detected and described as falling within the habitable zone of its star. A year later, Gliese 581g, a slightly less massive exoplanet belonging to the system, was announced as being another potentially habitable world. A few years later, though, further research indicated that the detection had been a glitch and the planets did not even exist. Analysis from 2015 showed that Gliese 581d probably does exist, although Gliese 581g is still debated. The Gliese 581 controversy exemplifies the uncertainties present in studying exoplanets, a branch of science that is still in its early stages.

CHAPTER FOUR

CONTINUING THE SEARCH

The year 2015 marked the twentieth anniversary of the discovery of the first exoplanet orbiting a sunlike star. In that time, new discoveries and breakthroughs have revolutionized scientists' conception of the celestial bodies that exist across the galaxy. In 1990, exoplanets were unknown. In 2015, extrapolating from data from the Kepler mission, a study found that billions of stars in the Milky Way probably have one to three planets in the habitable zone.

Ongoing discoveries and models will resolve some of the questions about the formation of planetary systems. Is the solar system truly atypical, as seems to be indicated by new discoveries, or will future observations reveal that

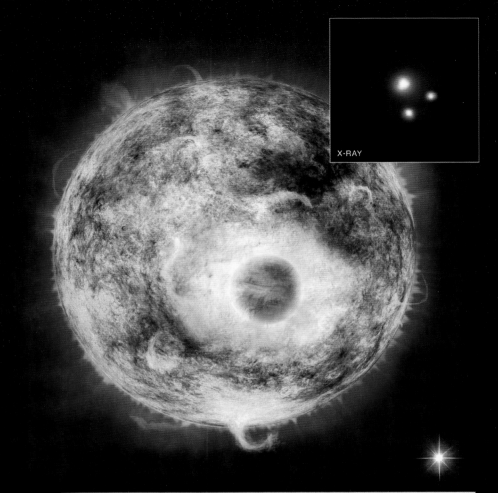

X-ray observations of HD 189733 b (top right), a hot Jupiter type gas giant, caught the exoplanet passing in front of its star. Artwork of the exoplanet shows the blue color caused by rainstorms of molten glass.

systems with a mix of small rocky planets and giants are common? Early on in the search for exoplanets, scientists thought that hot Jupiters were the most numerous type of planet. Now, it seems that super Earths are the dominant type. Future discoveries may cause scientists to revise their projected planetary census yet again.

Further research into the formation of the solar system could also increase understanding of the early interactions among planets, both around the sun and around faraway stars. For example, a computer model has shown that the motion of Jupiter could have affected the early development of the solar system. The model presents a mechanism explaining the absence of super Earths in the solar system. It depicts the giant planet sweeping inward

Scientists hypothesize about the life cycles of super Earth type planets such as Kepler-452b. Orbiting a star older than the sun, it could be experiencing a runaway greenhouse effect.

as the solar system formed, clearing out smaller planets before being pulled outward again by the force of Saturn's gravity. The inner planets formed later on.

Other new findings closer to home could be applicable as well. On Mars, the *Curiosity* rover is hunting for signs of life on the planet's surface, but it has no dedicated "life detection tool" because scientists do not know for sure what that would entail. *Curiosity*'s eventual discoveries could help inform the search for life on exoplanets. Exploration of the faraway moons of the solar systems will also produce new findings. NASA has proposed sending a probe to Europa, for example, and it would wield instruments that would determine the icy moon's composition and characteristics as well as measure the depth and salinity of its ocean. Deeper understanding of life in extreme environments on Earth could also help scientists predict different ways life could arise and evolve.

Development of new theoretical models could also expand conceptions of what life could look like on exoplanets. On planets without water, for example, life could evolve in alternate solvents such as dihydrogen or methane. Scientists have created a theoretical model of methane-based life that could exist on Saturn's moon Titan. It is made up of acrylonitrile, a type of hydrocarbon compound. It can organize itself into structures analogous to the protective membranes that encase the cells that make up Earth's life-forms.

ONGOING QUESTIONS

Falling within the habitable zone isn't enough to guarantee that a planet is truly habitable. For most confirmed exoplanets, though, little data is known other than a few basic measurements of their size and temperature. In the future, more information will be unveiled on factors such as composition and atmosphere, which will give a clearer idea of the planet's surface temperature. Presently, atmospheric composition has not been determined for most of the planets found by Kepler. Future observations of

An artist's conception shows exoplanet 51 Pegasi b crossing in front of the face of its star, as viewed from a hypothetical moon.

the exoplanets' spectra and even direct imaging will reveal whether some of these worlds are inhospitable or likely to be habitable. In 2015, scientists succeeded in obtaining a spectrum from the visible light of an exoplanet—51 Pegasi b—for the first time.

Today, however, even a mention of potential habitability in a scientific report can spark popular speculation about alien life-forms despite a lack of hard data. For example, a 2013 article on the pair of Kepler-62 exoplanets examined the potential for life evolving on a water world. The piece suggested that both aquatic organisms and winged creatures could exist, and it mentioned that advanced civilization might be less likely to develop in a world whose occupants couldn't use fire as a tool. All this speculation was based merely on a computer model suggesting that planets the same size as those particular exoplanets might be likely to exist as water worlds.

Some researchers have been giving serious thought to potential observational data that could indicate the presence of life. Spectra from

Astronomers believe that the super Earth type planet Kepler-62f, which falls within the habitable zone, is probably rocky and could possibly be a water world.

a planet's light can indicate biosignatures—traces of potential life. To figure out what compounds would serve as biomarkers, researchers examine the life processes on Earth that affect the composition of the atmosphere. The oxygen in the atmosphere today was originally produced over two billion years ago as a byproduct of bacterial activity. Microbes can also emit gases such as methane and nitrous oxide. If these types of compounds were ever detected in the atmosphere of an exoplanet, it would increase the probability that it harbors life based on similar organic processes to life on Earth.

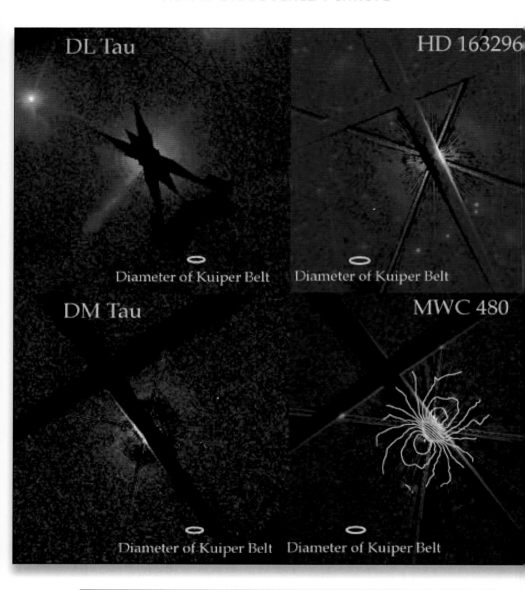

DL Tau

HD 163296

Diameter of Kuiper Belt

Diameter of Kuiper Belt

DM Tau

MWC 480

Diameter of Kuiper Belt

Diameter of Kuiper Belt

Images taken by the Hubble Space Telescope capture a key phase in planet formation. Matter surrounding newborn stars coalesces into disks that will eventually form planets.

Although such biosignatures have not been yet been observed, astronomers did discover complex organic molecules in the material surrounding a young star, MWC 480, in 2015. The star does not appear to have any planets.

In 2015, NASA announced the formation of NExSS (NASA Exoplanet System Science) to search for biosignatures on distant planets. The initiative brings together scientists from different institutions as well as different disciplines. These include Earth scientists, planetary scientists who study planets across the solar system, heliophysicists who study the sun, and astrophysicists who study exoplanets, stars, and other faraway objects. The initiative aims to describe possible environments beyond the solar system that might support life.

KEPLER CONTINUES

Analysis of the data from the original Kepler mission is ongoing. Astronomers are still in the process of confirming candidate planets, which number more than four thousand. A handful of

SETI: THE SEARCH FOR EXTRA-TERRESTRIAL INTELLIGENCE

It's conceivable that the first evidence of alien life will come not from a space probe, rover, or planet-hunting mission, but through the efforts of SETI—the search for extraterrestrial intelligence. SETI aims to detect signs of intelligent life outside of Earth. The first SETI efforts began in 1959 when a handful of astronomers hypothesized that intelligent aliens could communicate through radio waves, and that it could be possible for humans to detect the signals. Since then, numerous radio telescope projects have scanned the sky for potential transmissions. Astronomer Carl Sagan was a strong supporter of the search for extraterrestrial intelligence.

Today, a number of institutions conduct SETI projects. The SETI Institute, based in California, makes observations using radio and optical telescopes. SETI Institute scientists are also involved in NASA missions and other projects examining the nature of life in the universe. The University of California, Berkeley and Harvard University also conduct SETI research. In 1999, Berkeley launched the SETI@home project, in which people could volunteer their computing power by downloading a program that analyzes radio telescope data. No SETI search has yet confirmed the existence of extraterrestrial intelligence.

these are believed to be the nearest identifications yet to twin Earth type exoplanets, and most of the candidates are likely to be verified. NASA plans to finalize the catalog of Kepler findings in 2017.

The huge trove of data sent back from the original Kepler mission will likely serve as a valuable resource for scientists for many years to come. Researchers will develop new theories that call for an examination of Kepler's findings from a fresh angle. Advances in technology will allow for more extensive and in-depth statistical analysis of the massive amount of data collected by Kepler.

Meanwhile, the Kepler spacecraft is still hunting planets as it circles the sun, although the nature of the mission has been modified. After the failure of two of the craft's reaction wheels, engineers devised a means in which the pressure from the sun's radiation could be used as a third stabilizing force to balance the spacecraft. Kepler couldn't return to the original data-collecting mission because it no longer retained the necessary precision, but it could be pointed at a new set of targets.

In 2014, the new mission, named K2, was formally approved and funded by NASA. Instead of observing a single patch of sky, the spacecraft will view four to six different areas, switching its focus every two to three months. Its range is limited to the ecliptic plane, or the path across the sky traversed by the zodiac constellations. K2 will continue to search for exoplanets, as well as other objects such as star clusters, galaxies, and supernovae.

K2 observations lack the precision possible with the original setup, but they are still more precise than what is possible from the ground on Earth. The new mission began work in June 2014 and discovered its first exoplanet in December. HIP 116454 b is a new super Earth that is 2.5 times the size and 12 times the mass of Earth. The detection was made during a short test run of the new observation system. The first observation run began in May 2015. As of mid-2015, K2 had detected twenty-two exoplanets, which include a system consisting of a red dwarf orbited by three planets, one of which may fall within the habitable zone. The K2 mission will be funded through 2016 and could conceivably be extended if it continues to achieve useful scientific discoveries.

GETTING READY FOR THE NEXT DISCOVERIES

The Kepler mission produced milestone discoveries that might seem difficult to surpass, but scientists are already readying the next instruments and missions to study exoplanets. Several improved imagers have recently been installed in telescopes at some of the world's top observatories. The launch of new missions into space will also provide the opportunity to study exoplanets.

Kepler's successor mission is the Transiting Exoplanet Survey Satellite (TESS), scheduled by NASA for launch in 2017. Like Kepler, TESS will scan the sky using the transit detection method, seeking exoplanets ranging from the size of Earth to giants. The spacecraft will concentrate on examining smaller planets orbiting bright stars because it's easier to study

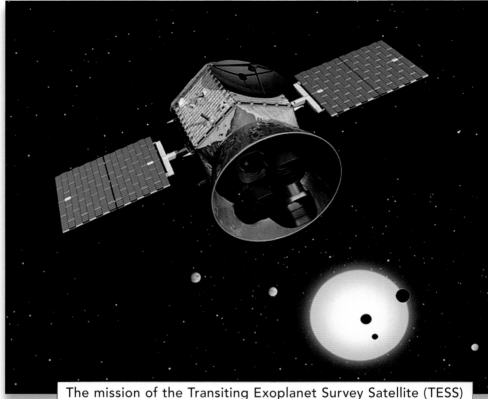

The mission of the Transiting Exoplanet Survey Satellite (TESS) will be to identify a list of the closest transiting planet systems, which will be targeted for follow-up studies.

the atmosphere and characteristics of brighter bodies. Unlike Kepler, TESS will survey the entire sky, not just a small area. The mission is expected to yield more than three thousand exoplanet candidates, including five hundred that are the twice the size of Earth or smaller. As with Kepler, the candidates will then be examined further with other telescopes based on Earth and in space.

The European Space Agency (ESA) is also planning exoplanet missions. The Characterising Exoplanet Satellite (CHEOPS), which is set to launch in 2017, will examine exoplanets that had been previously detected using ground-based methods. This mission will give astronomers the opportunity to learn more about exoplanets that are closer to Earth than most of the Kepler discoveries. The space telescope will yield much clearer images than were obtained on the ground. CHEOPS is intended to focus on exoplanets the size of Neptune and smaller.

The ESA plans to launch the larger Planetary Transits and Oscillations of Stars (PLATO) in 2024. Unlike other exoplanet missions, PLATO will include a range of detection instruments in its hunt for twin Earths.

NASA plans to launch the massive James Webb Space Telescope (JWST), intended to be the successor to the Hubble Space Telescope, in 2018. The JWST will be used to examine exoplanets as well as other objects in the solar system and beyond; it will not specialize in exo-

A full-scale model of the James Webb Space Telescope is displayed. The biggest space telescope ever to be constructed, it's as large as a tennis court and as tall as a four-story building.

planets like the Kepler mission. An infrared telescope, the JWST will be equipped with two instruments capable of searching for and examining exoplanets: the Near-Infrared Camera (NIRCam) and the Fine Guidance Sensor/ Near Infrared Imager and Slitless Spectrograph (FGS/NIRISS). The JWST's primary mirror, which will be made of lightweight beryllium, will have eighteen segments and can unfold and make adjustments after it has been launched. The JWST will search for exoplanets using the transit method, examine the spectra of exoplanetary atmospheres, and obtain direct images of exoplanets.

What about the more distant future? Will humans ever travel into space, meet aliens, and set foot on an exoplanet? NASA has been studying the feasibility of sending a manned mission to Mars. Humans may someday land on an asteroid. Scientists are more skeptical about the prospect of traveling light-years beyond Earth to another planetary system. Nonetheless, humans have achieved feats in the past that had once been described as impossible. Perhaps someday people will succeed in using an ion engine or an antimatter rocket to send a mission to an exoplanet.

GLOSSARY

ASTEROID A small, rocky planetary body. Most of the asteroids in the solar system orbit between Mars and Jupiter.

ATMOSPHERE The envelope of gases surrounding a celestial body.

COMET An object composed of ice and dust that orbits the sun.

CONSTELLATION A named pattern of stars in the sky.

ECCENTRIC Describing the extent that the shape of an orbit of a celestial body deviates from a perfect circle.

EVOLVE To change over time, especially from a simpler to a more complex form.

EXOPLANET A planet beyond the solar system.

EXTRATERRESTRIAL Originating or occurring outside Earth's atmosphere.

GALAXY A large grouping of millions or billions of stars held together by gravity.

GAS GIANT PLANET A massive planet made up mainly of gases such as hydrogen and helium, with no clearly defined surface.

GRAVITATIONAL MICROLENSING The brightening of a star when a celestial body passes between the star and an observer. Light from the star is bent and focused by gravity as the celestial body passes between the star and the observer on Earth. It is one of the methods used to discover exoplanets.

GRAVITY The physical force in nature that causes mutual attraction between two objects.

HABITABLE ZONE The range of distance around a star in which temperatures allow water to exist as a liquid.

HOT JUPITER A gas giant planet that orbits very close to its star.

HYDROTHERMAL Pertaining to the action of very hot water in Earth's crust.

INCIDENCE The rate or frequency of something occurring.

INFRARED Electromagnetic radiation having wavelengths longer than those of visible light.

LIGHT-YEAR The distance that light travels in a vacuum in one year, about 5.9 trillion miles (9.5 trillion km).

ORBIT The path taken by a celestial body revolving around another, such as a planet around a star.

PULSAR A dense, rapidly rotating star emitting bursts of energy.

RADIAL VELOCITY The speed or motion of a celestial body directed along a line toward or away from the observer.

ROVER A space vehicle that is designed to travel across and explore the surface of a planet or other celestial body.

SPECTRUM The bands of color produced when light is split up into its component wavelengths.

SUPER EARTH An exoplanet with a mass between one and ten times that of Earth.

SUPERNOVA The explosion of a massive star at the end of its life.

TRANSIT The passage of one celestial body in front of another, such as a planet before a star.

FOR MORE INFORMATION

American Astronomical Society (AAS)
2000 Florida Avenue NW, Suite 300
Washington, DC 20009-1231
(202) 328-2010
Website: http://aas.org

The major organization of professional astronomers in North America, the AAS aims to enhance and share humanity's scientific understanding of the universe.

Canadian Space Agency
John H. Chapman Space Centre
6767 Route de l'Aéroport
Saint-Hubert, QC J3Y 8Y9
Canada
(450) 926-4800
Website: http://www.asc-csa.gc.ca

The Canadian Space Agency coordinates all civil space-related policies and programs on behalf of the government of Canada.

European Space Agency (ESA)
8-10 rue Mario Nikis
75738 Paris Cedex 15
France
Website: http://www.esa.int/ESA

The ESA aims to shape the development of Europe's space capability and ensure that investment in space continues to deliver benefits to European citizens.

National Aeronautics and Space Administration (NASA)
Public Communications Office
NASA Headquarters
300 East Street SW, Suite 5R30
Washington, DC 20546
(202) 358-0001
Website: http://www.nasa.gov

NASA is the U.S. government agency that is responsible for the civilian space program as well as aeronautics and aerospace research. For information on its Exoplanet Exploration Program, see https://exep.jpl.nasa.gov.

The Planetary Society
85 South Grand Avenue
Pasadena, CA 91105
(626) 793-5100
Website: http://www.planetary.org

The Planetary Society was founded in 1980 by Carl Sagan, Bruce Murray, and Louis Friedman to inspire and involve the world's public in space exploration through advocacy, projects, and education.

SETI Institute
189 Bernardo Avenue, Suite 100
Mountain View, CA 94043
(650) 961-6633
Website: http://www.seti.org
The SETI Institute aims to explore, understand, and explain the origin and nature of life in the universe.

Smithsonian National Air and Space Museum
Independence Avenue at 6th Street SW
Washington, DC 20560
(202) 633-2214
Website: https://airandspace.si.edu
The National Air and Space Museum preserves and exhibits the world's largest collection of aviation and space artifacts.

WEBSITES

Due to the changing nature of Internet links, Rosen Publishing has developed an online list of Web sites related to the subject of this book. This site is updated regularly. Please use this link to access the list:
http://www.rosenlinks.com/SOE/Planet

FOR FURTHER READING

Aguilar, David A. *Alien Worlds: Your Guide to Extraterrestrial Life*. Washington, DC: National Geographic, 2013.

Aguilar, David A. *Space Encyclopedia: A Tour of Our Solar System and Beyond*. Washington, DC: National Geographic, 2013.

Carroll, Michael W. *Living Among Giants: Exploring and Settling the Outer Solar System*. New York, NY: Springer Verlag, 2014.

Dickinson, Terence. *Hubble's Universe: Greatest Discoveries and Latest Images*. New ed. Richmond Hill, ON: Firefly Books, 2014.

Dinwiddie, Robert. *The Planets*. New York, NY: DK Publishing, 2014.

Dinwiddie, Robert. *Universe*. Rev. ed. New York, NY: DK Publishing, 2012.

Encrenaz, Thérèse. *Planets: Ours and Others. From Earth to Exoplanets*. Hackensack, NJ: World Scientific Publishing Co., 2014.

Kallen, Stuart A. *The Search for Extraterrestrial Life*. San Diego, CA: ReferencePoint, 2012.

Kaufman, Marc. *Mars Up Close: Inside the Curiosity Mission*. Washington, DC: National Geographic, 2014.

Kops, Deborah. *Exploring Exoplanets*. Minneapolis, MN: Lerner Publications, 2012.

Meltzer, Michael. *The Cassini-Huygens Visit to Saturn: An Historic Mission to the Ringed Planet*. New York, NY: Springer Praxis Books, 2015.

Petersen, Carolyn Collins. *Astronomy 101: From the Sun and Moon to Wormholes and Warp Drive, Key Theories, Discoveries, and Facts About the Universe*. Avon, MA: F+W Media, Inc., 2013.

Sagan, Carl. *Contact*. New York, NY: Pocket Books, 1997.

Sagan, Carl. *Cosmos*. New York, NY: Ballantine Books, 2013.

Taylor, Fredric W. *The Scientific Exploration of Venus*. New York, NY: Cambridge University Press, 2014.

Trefil, James. *Space Atlas: Mapping the Universe and Beyond*. Washington, DC: National Geographic, 2012.

BIBLIOGRAPHY

Boss, Alan. *Looking for Earths: The Race to Find New Solar Systems*. New York, NY: Wiley, 1998.

California Institute of Technology. "NASA Exoplanet Archive." Retrieved June 23, 2015 (http://exoplanetarchive.ipac.caltech.edu/).

Casoli, Fabienne, and Thérèse Encrenaz. *The New Worlds: Extrasolar Planets*. New York, NY: Springer Praxis Books, 2007.

Chou, Felicia, and Laurie Cantillo. "NASA's Europa Mission Begins with Selection of Science Instruments." NASA. May 26, 2015. Retrieved June 23, 2015 (http://www.nasa.gov/press-release/nasa-s-europa-mission-begins-with-selection-of-science-instruments).

Crow, Diana. "Ultracold-Resistant Chemical on Titan Could Allow It to Harbor Life." *Scientific American*, March 3, 2015. Retrieved June 23, 2015 (http://www.scientificamerican.com/article/ultracold-resistant-chemical-on-titan-could-allow-it-to-harbor-life/).

Drake, Nadia. "Explosion in Planet Discoveries Intensifies Search for Life Beyond Earth." *National Geographic*, May 9, 2014. Retrieved June 23, 2015 (http://news.nationalgeographic.com/news/2014/05/140509-exoplanets-earth-life-science-exploration-space/).

ESA. "Was Venus Once a Habitable Planet?" June 24, 2010. Retrieved June 23, 2015 (http://www.esa.int/

Our_Activities/Space_Science/Venus_Express/
Was_Venus_once_a_habitable_planet).

Finkbeiner, Ann. "Planets in Chaos: The Discovery of Thousands of Star Systems Wildly Different from Our Own Has Demolished Ideas About How Planets Form." *Nature*, July 2, 2014. Retrieved June 23, 2015 (http://www.nature.com/news/astronomy-planets-in-chaos-1.15480).

Grush, Loren. "For the First Time, Visible Light from an Exoplanet Detected." *Popular Science*, April 23, 2015. Retrieved June 23, 2015 (http://www.popsci.com/we-now-know-how-measure-visible-light-reflecting-exoplanets).

Hall, Shannon. "Three Exoplanet Molds: Metals Matter." *Sky and Telescope*, June 3, 2014. Retrieved June 23, 2015 (http://www.skyandtelescope.com/astronomy-news/three-exoplanet-molds-metals-matter/).

Herkewitz, William. "Why the Warm Ocean on This Moon of Saturn Could Be Perfect for Life." *Popular Mechanics*, March 11, 2015. Retrieved June 23, 2015 (http://www.popularmechanics.com/space/deep-space/a14507/enceladus-saturn-moon-ocean/).

Howell, Elizabeth. "Microbes Can Survive In Meteorites If Shielded from UV Radiation, Study Says." *Astrobiology Magazine*, May 28, 2015.

Retrieved June 23, 2015 (http://www.astrobio.net/
topic/origins/extreme-life/microbes-can-survive-in-
meteorites-if-shielded-from-uv-radiation-study-says/).

Jayawardhana, Ray. *Strange New Worlds: The Search
for Alien Planets and Life Beyond Our Solar System.*
Princeton, NJ: Princeton University Press, 2011.

Jenkins, Ann, and Ray Villard. "NASA's Hubble Observations Suggest Underground Ocean on Jupiter's
Largest Moon." HubbleSite, March 12, 2015.
Retrieved June 23, 2015 (http://hubblesite.org/
newscenter/archive/releases/2015/09/full/).

Kasting, James. *How to Find a Habitable Planet.* Princeton, NJ: Princeton University Press, 2010.

Kitchin, Chris. *Exoplanets: Finding, Exploring, and
Understanding Alien Worlds.* New York, NY:
Springer, 2012.

Klotz, Irene. "Jupiter May Have Killed Solar System's
Baby Super-Earths." *Discovery News*, March 23,
2015. Retrieved June 23, 2015 (http://news
.discovery.com/space/jupiter-cleared-out-
neighborhood-for-earth-150323.htm).

Lemonick, Michael D. "A Living Ocean on a Jovian
Moon?" *Time*, March 15, 2013. Retrieved June 23,
2015 (http://science.time.com/2013/03/15/a-living-
ocean-on-a-jovian-moon/).

Lemonick, Michael D. *Mirror Earth: The Search for Our
Planet's Twin.* New York, NY: Bloomsbury, 2013.

Lovett, Richard A. "Three Theories of Planet Formation Busted, Expert Says." *National Geographic
News*, February 22, 2011. Retrieved June 23,
2015 (http://news.nationalgeographic.com/
news/2011/02/110222-planets-formation-
theory-busted-earth-science-space/).

NASA. "Cassini Solstice Mission." Retrieved June 23,
2015 (http://saturn.jpl.nasa.go).

NASA. "James Webb Space Telescope." Retrieved
June 23, 2015 (http://www.jwst.nasa.gov/).

NASA. "Kepler and K2 Missions." Retrieved June 23,
2015 (http://www.nasa.gov/mission_pages/kepler/
main/index.html).

NASA. "Solar System Exploration." Retrieved June 23,
2015 (http://solarsystem.nasa.gov/index.cfm).

NASA. "TESS: Transiting Exoplanet Survey Satellite."
Retrieved June 23, 2015 (http://tess.gsfc.nasa.
gov/).

Niels Bohr Institute, University of Copenhagen. "Planets in the Habitable Zone Around Most Stars, Cal-
culate Researchers." March 18, 2015. Retrieved
June 23, 2015 (http://www.nbi.ku.dk/english/news/
news15/planets-in-the-habitable-zone-around-
most-stars-calculate-researchers/).

Overbye, Dennis. "Astronomers Have Found an Ana-
logue for the Earth." *New York Times*, July 24,
2015.

Overbye, Dennis. "NASA Says Data Reveals Kepler 452b, an Earth-Like Planet." *New York Times*, July 23, 2015.

Overbye, Dennis. "So Many Earth-Like Planets, So Few Telescopes." *New York Times*, January 6, 2015.

Redd, Nola Taylor. "Basic Ingredients for Life Found Around Distant Star." SPACE.com. April 8, 2015. Retrieved June 23, 2015 (http://www.space.com/29049-life-ingredients-found-around-star.html).

Seager, Sara. "The Future of Spectroscopic Life Detection on Exoplanets." PNAS, September 2, 2014. Retrieved June 23, 2015 (http://www.pnas.org/content/111/35/12634).

Stromberg, Joseph. "Can We Power a Space Mission to an Exoplanet?" Smithsonian.com. June 28, 2013. Retrieved June 23, 2015 (http://www.smithsonianmag.com/science-nature/can-we-power-a-space-mission-to-an-exoplanet-3948923/?no-ist).

Swain, Mark. "Probing the Atmospheres of Exoplanets." *Hubble 2008: Science Year in Review*. NASA Goddard Space Flight Center and the Space Telescope Science Institute. 2008.

Wall, Mike. "Signs of Alien Life Will Be Found by 2025, NASA's Chief Scientist Predicts." Space.com. April 07, 2015. Retrieved June 23, 2015 (http://

www.space.com/29041-alien-life-evidence-by-2025-nasa.html).

Wall, Mike. "What Might Alien Life Look Like on New 'Water World' Planets?" Space.com. April 18, 2013 (http://www.space.com/20728-new-alien-planets-oceans-life.html).

Woo, Marcus. "Astronomers Get Closer Than Ever in the Hunt for Earth's Twin." *Wired*, January 6, 2015. Retrieved June 23, 2015 (http://www.wired.com/2015/01/kepler-new-planets-Earth-size-habitable-zone-aas/).

Woods Hole Oceanographic Institution. "Hydrothermal Vents." Retrieved June 23, 2015 (http://www.whoi.edu/main/topic/hydrothermal-vents).

INDEX

ABOUT THE AUTHOR

Corona Brezina has written over a dozen young adult books. Several of her previous works have also focused on topics related to science and technology, including *Discovering Relativity* (The Scientist's Guide to Physics) and *Marc Andreessen* (Tech Pioneers). She lives in Chicago, Illinois.

PHOTO CREDITS